Alternative Assets and Public Pension Plan Performance

Douglas Robertson and Ellen Wielezynski

Office of the Comptroller of the Currency

OCC Economics Working Paper 2008-2 August 2008

JEL Classifications: G11, G23 Keywords: Alternative Investments, Pension Funds

The opinions in this paper are those of the authors and do not necessarily reflect those of the Office of the Comptroller of the Currency or the Treasury Department. The authors thank David Nebhut, Gary Whalen, John Karikari, and seminar participants at the Office of the Comptroller of the Currency for helpful comments and Frank Dwyer for editorial assistance.

Corresponding Author: Douglas Robertson, Mail Stop 2-4, Office of the Comptroller of the Currency, 250 E Street, SW, Washington, DC 20219
Douglas.Robertson@occ.treas.gov

Alternative Assets and Public Pension Plan Performance

Abstract

As public pension plans steer more of their portfolios toward alternative assets such as hedge funds, private equity funds, and real estate, we examine how these investments have affected public pension plan performance. We find somewhat mixed results. When compared to pension plans with smaller allocations, public pension plans with at least 10 percent of their assets allocated to alternative investments had significantly higher annual returns in 2004, 2005, and 2006. However, these same plans had lower returns, though not significantly so, in 2002 and 2003. We also find that pension plans that began investing in alternative assets as early as 2001 did not significantly outperform pension plans that began investing in these assets after 2001. This result suggests that much of the performance benefit of alternative assets may be due to superior returns over just the past three years. Turning to risk, we find that pension plans that invested in alternative assets, regardless of the size of the allocation, had significantly higher standard deviations in their returns over a five-year period relative to other pension plans. Measuring risk-adjusted returns with the Sharpe Ratio, we find no significant differences between pension plans that invested in alternative assets and those that did not.

We also explore whether hedge fund investments in particular affected performance. Because hedge funds are new investments for public pension plans and only a few plans invest in them, we need more seasoned data before being able to come to any strong conclusions regarding the effect of hedge funds on pension plan performance. However, based on our current data, we found no significant difference in investment returns for public pension plans with hedge fund investments in 2006.

Alternative Assets and Public Pension Plan Performance

I. Introduction

Pension plans, which invest in a broad range of assets, increasingly invest in alternative assets such as hedge funds, real estate, and private equity funds. The rapid growth of the largely unregulated hedge fund industry, the air of mystery surrounding hedge fund investments, and the impressive speed with which some of these funds have imploded have all helped to raise the level of scrutiny directed at hedge funds. This scrutiny has extended to the relationship between pension funds and hedge funds, and has raised questions regarding the wisdom of including hedge funds in pension fund portfolios.

These questions arise from the fact that while most pension funds easily qualify to invest in hedge funds, the ultimate beneficiaries of the pension plans typically do not.[1] Most pension plans easily surpass the threshold of $5 million in assets necessary for employee benefit plans to invest in hedge funds. However, the beneficiaries of these pension funds (teachers, police officers, firefighters, and other wage earners) for the most part do not meet either the net worth or the annual income thresholds, and therefore cannot invest in hedge funds. As pension fund investments in hedge funds increase, the question becomes how hedge funds and other "alternative investments" have affected recent pension fund performance.

---

[1] Securities and Exchange Commission regulations effectively restrict hedge fund sales to "accredited investors" and "qualified purchasers." Accredited investors include (1) individuals or married couples with a net worth exceeding $1 million; (2) individuals or married couples with an income exceeding $200,000 or $300,000 respectively, in each of the past two years and an expectation of the same in the current year; and (3) employee benefit plans with total assets in excess of $5 million. Qualified purchasers include individuals with $5 million or more in investments and businesses with discretion over $25 million or more in investments.

We address this question by examining a sample of public pension plans and comparing average investment returns, the variance of these returns, and the risk-adjusted returns of plans grouped according to their target asset allocations. We find that although only a few public pension plans in our sample currently invest in hedge funds, there is no significant difference between investment returns for the pension plans that had hedge fund investments greater than zero in 2006 and those that did not. However, we get very different results when the definition of alternative assets includes such investments as real estate and private equity.[2]

Compared to pension plans with smaller alternative asset allocations, pension funds that invest at least 10 percent of their portfolio in alternative assets had significantly higher annual returns in 2004, 2005, and 2006. However, these same plans had lower returns, though not significantly so, in 2002 and 2003. When we subdivide the 22 pension plans that had at least a 10 percent alternative asset allocation in 2006 according to whether they had such an allocation as early as 2001 or not, there is no significant difference in returns over the periods we examine. This result suggests that much of the performance benefit of alternative assets may be due to superior returns over just the past three years.

In conducting our tests, we sequentially compare mean investment returns for a range of asset allocation targets. Not surprisingly, our results with respect to significant differences in investment returns depend somewhat on the size of the target allocation for alternative assets. While statistical significance sometimes varies with the size of the target allocation, whether returns were higher or lower in a particular year did not change.

---

[2] See Brinson, Hood, and Beebower (1986) and Tokat, Wicas, and Kinniry (2006) for discussions of the importance of asset allocation decisions in determining portfolio performance.

Pension plans with alternative asset target allocations greater than zero had lower returns in 2002 and 2003 and higher returns in 2004, 2005, and 2006. These higher returns over the past three years also lifted the 3-year, 5-year, and 10-year average returns for pensions investing in alternative assets above those that did not.

As one might expect, alternative assets, while often generating higher returns, appear to introduce greater risk into the portfolio. When we look at risk, as measured by the standard deviations of returns over a five-year period, we find that pension funds investing in alternative assets had significantly higher standard deviations, regardless of the size of the target allocation for alternative assets. These risk and return tradeoffs offset each other when we look at risk-adjusted returns using the Sharpe Ratio. Looking at excess returns and standard deviations over a five-year period, there is no significant difference in Sharpe Ratios between pensions that invest in alternative assets and those that do not.

Because hedge funds are relatively new investments and only a few public pension plans currently hold them, we need more seasoned data before being able to come to any strong conclusions regarding the effect of hedge funds on public pension plans. Nonetheless, our results regarding the performance tradeoffs of broadly defined alternative investments provide some insight into how investments in hedge funds, private equity funds, and real estate combined have affected pension plan performance.

Our brief time series of pension plan data shows the growing prevalence of alternative assets in public pension plan portfolios. Alternative investments comprise an important investment class for many pension funds. While our results suggest that alternative assets do not immunize pension plans against the risk-return paradigm, their hefty returns over the three years ending in 2006 may help explain the rush to these assets. Nevertheless, the potential risks and limited history of these assets highlight the extreme importance of disclosure and due diligence for pension fund fiduciaries that elect to plunge into the opaque pool of alternative investments.

The rest of this paper begins with a brief discussion of some of the issues surrounding pension funds and alternative investments. After describing the pension fund data we gathered and our empirical findings, we present our conclusions and the possible policy implications of our results.

II. Alternative Investments and Public Pension Funds

Although public pension funds only recently began investing in hedge funds, many public pension funds have long been investors in other alternative investments. Such investments include private equity, real estate, foreign currencies, derivatives, and in some cases, timber. Thus, we use the term alternative investments to refer broadly to assets other than domestic and international stocks and fixed-income assets.

An investment oversight council generally determines the composition of public portfolios by setting asset allocation targets. These councils often have a great deal of flexibility regarding the types of investments they may approve.[3] The investment policies of some pension plans set a specific allocation target for hedge funds, while other pension plans simply indicate that hedge funds are an appropriate investment within the

---

[3] Pension fund managers also have some discretion in meeting asset allocation targets. Target allocations are often expressed as permissible ranges. While investment oversight councils choose target allocations, fund managers select specific investments. In general, the investment oversight council and the executive management of the retirement system are fiduciaries of the pension.

category of alternative assets.[4] Table 1 shows three examples of asset allocation targets. The examples in table 1 reflect the typical public pension fund allocation — heavy weighting toward equities and fixed income investments and smaller allocations for real estate and alternative assets.

While some pension fund experts herald incorporating hedge fund investments in pension fund portfolios,[5] others are more nervous about the idea of workers' pension plans investing in such risky assets.[6] Advocates of hedge funds point to the non-correlation of hedge fund returns with stock market returns, portfolio diversification, and the potential for higher returns. Skeptics of hedge funds cite their eye-popping fees, lack of government oversight, limited disclosure, and spectacular failures, including Amaranth in 2006 and Long Term Capital Management in 1998.

Concerns regarding pensions investing in hedge funds touches on the broader question of what investments are appropriate for pension funds. Ultimately, a pension fund's fiduciaries are responsible for defining appropriate investments. In the case of public pension funds, state or local statute will sometimes direct fiduciaries regarding permissible investments, but in general a plan's fiduciaries set investment policy. Maggs (2006) reports on several states enacting legislation in the past few years to allow the state pension fund to invest in alternative investments. Maggs points out that these

---

[4] The State Employees' Retirement System of Illinois and the Missouri State Employees' Retirement System are examples of pension plans that have set specific allocation target for hedge funds. The California Public Employees' Retirement System is an example of a fund that lists hedge funds as an acceptable investment within the alternative asset category.
[5] See Gregoriou and Rouah (2002).
[6] See Mary Williams Walsh and Riva D. Atlas, "Pension, hedge-fund ties a concern," *The Seattle Times*, November 27, 2005. Also, the Congressional Research Service reports that in March 2007, Senators Max Baucus and Charles Grassley asked the Government Accountability Office (GAO) "to investigate the benefits and risks that hedge funds pose to pension funds and their participants." See William Klunk, "Pension Funds Investing in Hedge Funds," Congressional Research Service, June 15, 2007.

decisions to move into alternative assets are often in response to poor investment returns and increasing deficits in the pension plan.[7]

Many of the questions that pension plan fiduciaries must address regarding hedge fund investments apply to other alternative investments as well. Steenburg and Maggs (2007) discuss many of the concerns fiduciaries have about hedge fund investments. They point out that fiduciaries considering hedge fund investments have to confront potential problems arising from a lack of transparency and the accompanying possibility of fraud, the greater risk that comes with greater leverage, new areas of risk such as counterparty risk that may be difficult to quantify, lagging information about a fund's risk exposure, and liquidity issues related to lockup provisions. Private equity and real estate investments often pose a similar set of problems for fiduciaries. As we show in the next section, fiduciaries and the public pension plans for which they are responsible have been willing to accept these challenges and venture into alternative investments.

III. Public Pension Fund Data

In order to analyze the role of hedge funds and alternative investments in pension plans, we examine the asset allocation targets and subsequent performance of a sample of public employee pension plans. We gathered data from a large public employee pension system in each of the 50 states and the District of Columbia.[8] Together, these 51 defined benefit pension plans hold approximately $1.7 trillion in assets and cover more than 13 million plan members.

---

[7] See Brull (2007) for a description of the difficulties the University of California's pension fund encountered after the 2000 bear market. Denmark (2007) states that university endowments moved into alternative investments because of stock market losses around the year 2000.
[8] In selecting these plans, we chose the statewide public employees retirement system whenever available.

For each of the 51 pension plans, we gathered information on total assets, total membership, the most recent target asset allocations, allocation targets in 2001, the 2006 market value of investments, and investment returns over several periods. Table 2 provides some summary statistics on our sample of pension plans.

As table 2 indicates, most public pension funds now invest in real estate and other alternative investments in addition to equity and fixed income assets.[9] But only nine plans show a separate accounting item for hedge funds in either their statement of plan assets or their schedule of plan investments. As mentioned earlier, because some pension plans simply include hedge funds within the alternative investment category, the number of pension plans in our sample that invest in hedge funds may be higher than the nine indicated in table 2. Only six pension plans reported owning neither real estate nor alternative investments.[10]

In order to determine how asset allocation targets have changed over recent years, we gathered the allocation targets in 2001 and 2006 for each of the pension plans in our sample. Table 3 provides a summary of these target allocations, where the mean targets and standard deviations are for pension plans with a target greater than zero in that asset category. As table 3 suggests, all 51 pension plans allocated the largest portion of their portfolio to equity and fixed income investments in 2001 and 2006.

The information in table 3 reveals several changes in asset allocation targets between 2001 and 2006. The number of pension plans in our sample allocating assets to either real estate or other alternative investments increased from 37 in 2001 to 45 in 2006.

---

[9] All 51 pension plans have equity and fixed income investments; however, one pension fund did not provide dollar values for individual asset categories. Thus, investment values for specific assets in table 2 are out of a total of 50 pension funds rather than 51.

[10] The six pension plans without real estate or alternative investments in 2006 are from Georgia, New Mexico, Oklahoma, South Carolina, Texas, and West Virginia.

Pension plans investing in real estate increased from 31 in 2001 to 36 in 2006, and plans with other alternative investments increased from 32 to 36 over the same period. By 2006, nearly all public pension plans in our sample target at least some investments in either real estate or other alternative investments. Although more public pension funds now target real estate and alternative investments, the average target allocation for each of these classes increased only slightly. Also, whereas there were no specific hedge fund target allocations in 2001, by 2006 seven public pension plans had an explicit target for hedge fund investments. Table 3 also shows that the increased allocation for hedge funds and alternative investments generally came at the expense of fixed income investment targets, which decreased from 35 percent to 30 percent.[11]

To compare the investment performance of different pension funds, we gathered information on investment returns from 2002 through 2006 as well as 3-year, 5-year, and 10-year averages.[12] For a comparison of investment returns to make sense, the returns have to cover the same time period. Most pension plans in our study use fiscal years ending with June 30, so we limit our comparisons to the 39 plans in our sample with that fiscal year. Table 4 provides a summary of the net investment returns for those 39 plans.[13] While investment returns were strong for the three years ending in 2006, weaker returns for the five- and ten-year averages reflect the largely negative returns in 2001 and 2002. Those years of negative returns may have helped to send pension managers off in search of potentially higher returns through alternative investments.

[11] Recent media reports suggest that the trend toward more alternative assets is continuing. The Washington State Investment Board recently increased their alternative asset allocation to 38 percent. See Brull (2008).

[12] Returns are annual returns net of investment management fees. Ippolito and Turner (1987) study the effect of turnover and fees in pension plans. Although they find evidence that private pension plans underperformed the S&P 500 and mutual funds, they find no evidence that fees or portfolio turnover accounted for the poor performance.

[13] As the sample size column in table 4 indicates, not all pension plans reported 10-year returns.

To understand how various assets contributed to pension fund returns during our sample period, we look at a summary of investment results from one of the pension systems in our sample. Table 5 summarizes benchmark investment results from the North Dakota Public Employees Retirement System 2006 annual report. As table 5 shows, after weakening overall returns in 2002 and 2003, domestic equities performed very well in 2004 and continued to deliver at or near double-digit returns in 2005 and 2006. Like domestic equities, international equities dragged down overall returns in 2002, but then provided spectacular returns from 2004 through 2006. Real estate and private equity also had high returns in 2005 and 2006. Fixed income returns were relatively strong in 2002 and 2003 and relatively weak in 2004 and 2006. By looking at these investment results, we can surmise that pensions heavily weighted toward fixed income assets were likely to do well in 2002 and 2003, and relatively poorly in 2004 and 2006. Similarly, pensions with large allocations for domestic and international equities fared worse in 2002 and better from 2004 through 2006, especially those pensions with sizeable allocations for international equities.

We see these relative performance expectations borne out when we compare total portfolio returns of pensions grouped on either side of the median target allocation for each particular asset. Table 6 shows the difference in returns and the p-value across our four major asset categories for each return period in our data set. Somewhat surprisingly, pensions with domestic equity target allocations above the median had lower returns in every period except 2004. However, although many of the return differences were close to being significant at the 5 percent level, only the five-year average return difference is significant. Allocations above the median for international equities led to higher returns in each of our periods. These higher returns were statistically significant in 2004 and 2005 as well as for the three-year and five-year averages ending in 2006.

Table 6 also shows that a fixed income allocation above the median resulted in significantly different returns in each year from 2002 through 2006 and for the three-year average. These returns were significantly higher in 2002 and 2003, but significantly lower in 2004, 2005, and 2006. Pensions with an allocation above the median in alternative assets had lower returns in 2002 and 2003, but significantly higher returns every other period. It is interesting to note that the set of pensions with an alternative asset allocation above the median target is the only group to have a significantly different ten-year average return. We now look more closely at the role of alternative assets in pension plan performance.

IV. Performance Comparison of Public Pension Funds

In performing our analysis, we combine real estate, hedge funds, and alternative investments and refer to this combined asset category as alternative investments. To analyze how alternative investments may have affected portfolio performance, we first use a two-sided t-test to compare mean investment returns of pension plans with varying percentages of assets dedicated to alternative investments. For instance, in our first test we compare mean investment returns of pension plans with alternative asset allocation targets greater than zero to plans with no target for these assets. We then proceed to examine the results of t-tests comparing mean returns as we increase the alternative investment allocation target that separates our two groups. Often, investment comparisons evaluate performance relative to a market portfolio with a similar level of risk.[14] Our performance evaluation is relative to other pension plans with similar actuarial objectives.

After comparing groups based on 2006 target asset allocations, we make comparisons according to 2006 hedge fund investments as well as joint 2001 and 2006 alternative asset allocations. For each comparison, we group pension plans according to whether their target allocation for alternative investments exceeds the threshold for that comparison. Threshold target allocations are zero percent, 5 percent, 10 percent, 15 percent, and 20 percent. However, as our basic results are the same at 5, 10, and 15 percent thresholds, we only report results for the zero, 10, and 20 percent thresholds. As part of the diagnostic check for the t-test, we run an F-test to determine if the two groups have equal variance. In addition to allowing us to determine the appropriate t-test to perform, this equality of variance test reveals whether or not a higher return comes at the price of greater volatility within the group, one aspect of our examination of risk.[15]

Performance Comparison by 2006 Target Asset Allocations

Our first set of performance comparisons groups pension plans based on their 2006 target allocation for alternative investments. Starting with a zero threshold, we compare investment returns for the 34 plans with a 2006 allocation target for alternative investments that was greater than zero versus the five plans that did not target alternative investments. Table 7a shows the results of this first comparison. For each group it shows

---

[14] See Fama (1972). Blake, Lehmann and Timmermann (1999) point out in their study of pension plans in the United Kingdom that performance evaluations distinguishing between short-term market timing decisions and long-term strategic asset allocation decisions may also be desirable. In this study, we do not try to distinguish how these different decisions might be affecting returns.
[15] Ackermann, McEnally, and Ravenscraft (1999) use a similar approach in their study of hedge fund performance. They point out that using annual rather than monthly returns may smooth large variations in monthly returns. Given the long investment horizon of pension funds, this smoothed annual return variance may be a better measure of risk for pension plans.

the number of pension plans reporting returns for the given time period, the mean investment return for that period, and the standard deviation. The table also shows the differences between the group means, the p-value of the group t-test to determine if the mean returns for the two groups are significantly different, and the probability of exceeding the critical value of the F-test to determine if the variances of the returns for the two groups are significantly different.[16]

As table 7a shows, although the sample size of pension plans with no alternative investment allocations in 2006 is quite small, the p-values indicate significantly different investment returns in four out of five years. Pensions with alternative asset allocations had significantly higher returns in 2004 and 2006 as well as higher returns, though not significantly so, in 2005. However, these plans had significantly lower returns in 2002 and 2003. At the longer time horizons of five and ten years, we find no significant difference in the investment returns of the two groups, although pensions with alternative assets had nominally higher returns than those without alternative assets.

The column in table 7a showing the differences in the means reveals that these differences in average portfolio returns are indeed often substantial. Pensions with alternative assets had returns that were 310 basis points higher for the 12 months ending June 30, 2004, 313 basis points higher for the 12 months ending June 30, 2006, and 260 basis points higher for the annual average over the three years ending in June 2006. Similarly, when returns were lower, they were considerably lower: 336 basis points lower in 2002 and 150 basis points lower in 2003. At the five- and 10-year horizon, the

---

[16] In reporting significance, we use a level of significance of .05.

14

differences are statistically insignificant and nominally much smaller: 45 basis points over the five years ending in June 2006 and only 31 basis points over the 10-year span.[17]

Did those higher returns come at the price of greater volatility? We look at this question of risk in several ways. Later we will discuss the variability of returns over five years at individual pension plans, but for now we look only at the within-group variability of returns. We conduct F tests to compare the variances of the returns of the two groups of pension plans, those with alternative asset allocations and those without. According to these tests, the two groups do not exhibit different return variance. As shown in the last column in table 7a, in all but one case we do not have sufficient evidence to reject the hypothesis of equal variance. The equality of variance test of the 10-year returns is the one instance where the sample variances of the two groups are significantly different. However, we have to discount this result due to the extremely small sample size of pension plans with no alternative assets that reported 10-year average returns.[18] Thus, according to most of the equality of variances tests, pension funds investing in alternative assets had the same volatility as pension funds without alternative investments, as measured by within-group sample variance.

We next look at how these group mean and variance results change as we increase the alternative asset allocation threshold. Table 7b shows the return comparisons between 22 pension plans with an alternative asset target allocation of at least 10 percent versus 17 plans with a target allocation of less than 10 percent. Comparing the mean

---

[17] We use target allocations to determine our groupings rather than actual June 30 portfolio shares because the June 30 figures represent only a snapshot of asset allocations. Nevertheless, we conducted our return comparisons using actual dollar allocations and had nearly identical results. We report these results using actual portfolio shares in tables 15a through 15c. Table 15c uses the 15 percent threshold because only one pension had alternative assets that comprised at least 20 percent of the portfolio in 2006.
[18] Because we reject the hypothesis of equal variance for 10-year returns, we use the Satterthwaite method t-test as opposed to the usual pooled method. The use of the Satterthwaite method for the t-test occurs throughout this study when we reject the hypothesis of equal variance.

returns of these two groups, we find that the pension plans with the larger alternative asset allocation target had significantly higher returns than other pension plans at most of our time horizons. These significantly higher returns ranged from 76 basis points for the 10-year average return to 303 basis points in 2006. Pensions with the higher alternative asset target had lower returns in 2002 and 2003, but the differences (69 and 84 basis points, respectively) are not statistically significant. As with our earlier results, we find in most instances that the variance of the returns is not significantly different between the two groups.

As we continue to increase the alternative asset threshold that separates the two groups, we find that the tenor of the results remains the same although statistical significance fluctuates somewhat. When the alternative asset target increases to 20 percent or more, we find that mean return differences remain significant only for the years 2005 and 2006 as well as the 3-year and 5-year averages. However, as we see across tables 7a through 7c, whether the return differences are positive or negative remains constant though significance may change.

Overall, these results suggest that public pension funds that allocate at least 10 percent of their assets to alternative assets enjoyed large and significant return premiums for the three years ending in 2006. However, lower returns in 2002 and 2003 remind us that alternative assets may not always prove to be a pension's panacea. Certainly it would be helpful to see these results sustained over a longer sample period before giving alternative asset target allocations between 10 percent and 20 percent the strong endorsement these return results suggest. Of course, investment returns are just one component of pension fund performance. Risk also plays an important part.

Risk and Risk-adjusted Returns

Risk, as measured by the variability of investment returns, is an important component of pension fund performance. We have already looked at one aspect of risk by examining the equality of variances across our pension groupings. This examination revealed that, for the most part, return variances between the two groups are not significantly different from each other. In other words, the return premiums enjoyed in 2006 by pension plans targeting alternative assets did not occur because a few funds had astronomical returns to offset dismal returns at several other funds within the same group. Rather, our group variance results show that there is generally no significant difference in the way pensions in each group cluster around their respective mean returns.

That is one way to look at risk, but from the perspective of the individual pension plans, perhaps a more critical measure of risk is the variability of returns in each portfolio over time. We look at this aspect of risk by comparing the standard deviations of investment returns over our brief sample period, from 2002 through 2006. Table 8 shows the results of these comparisons across five alternative asset thresholds, from zero percent to 20 percent. Consistently across the different thresholds, we find significantly higher standard deviations in investment returns for pensions targeting alternative assets. Returns at pension funds with higher target allocations for alternative assets had significantly higher variances over our five-year sample period. Thus, according to this common measure of portfolio risk, portfolios investing in alternative assets are riskier than portfolios that allocate less toward alternative assets.

To what extent, then, do risk and return offset each other? We investigate this question by examining risk-adjusted returns as measured by the Sharpe Ratio. The Sharpe Ratio is a return-to-risk ratio calculated as the average portfolio return premium divided by the standard deviation of that return premium. The return premium is the difference between the portfolio return and a benchmark; in our case we use the return on 90-day T-bills as our risk-free benchmark. In order to test for differences in risk-adjusted returns, we then test for differences in mean Sharpe Ratios between our pensions grouped according to alternative asset targets. Table 9 shows the results of these comparisons across five alternative asset thresholds using our returns from 2002 through 2006. As table 9 shows, consistently across the different thresholds, we do not find evidence of any significant differences in Sharpe Ratios. This suggests that on a risk-adjusted basis, there is no difference in the performance of the pension plans in our sample regardless of the size of their alternative asset allocation.

Performance Comparison by 2001 and 2006 Target Asset Allocations

Perhaps not surprisingly, our results from grouping pensions according to their 2006 target allocations clearly suggest that portfolio allocations affect investment returns. Given these results, we are also interested in determining whether an early adoption of an allocation target for alternative investments has had an effect on fund performance. Before concluding that investing in alternative assets brought higher returns in recent years, it would be meaningful to see some evidence of these results persisting over an extended period of time. With the data currently available, we can explore the effect of long-term investments in alternative assets by jointly using 2001 and 2006 target asset allocations to determine our pension plan groupings for performance comparisons.

If investing in alternative assets carries benefits over the long-term, we would like to see some evidence of superior performance from pension plans that have dedicated assets to alternative investments for a longer period of time. Here we find mixed evidence of this long-term accomplishment. First we compare pension plans that met the same alternative asset allocation threshold in 2001 and 2006 against pension plans that did not meet the same threshold in both years.[19] Then we subdivide the subset of pensions that met the 10 percent threshold for alternative assets in 2006 according to whether they also met that threshold in 2001.

The first approach, grouping pension plans that met the allocation threshold in both years, allows us to examine the investment performance of pension plans with a more extended record of investing in alternative assets. Tables 10a through 10c show the results from these performance comparisons at various allocation thresholds. Comparing mean returns shows several differences relative to the results when using only 2006 allocation targets. Table 10a shows that pension plans allocating assets toward alternative investments in 2001 and 2006 only had significantly higher returns in 2006 and over the three years ending in 2006. Looking back at table 7a, which just used the 2006 allocation target, 2002, 2003, and 2004 had significantly different returns. Of course, in two of those years, 2002 and 2003, pensions investing in alternatives had significantly lower returns. Using the 2001 and 2006 targets, pensions with alternative

---

[19] Target allocations do not have to be equal in 2001 and 2006 because our thresholds cover a range and the specific target allocation can increase without affecting the grouping. For instance, if a plan had an alternative asset target of 11 percent in 2001 and 14 percent or even 20 percent in 2006, it meets the 10 percent threshold in both years and will be grouped accordingly.

assets still had lower returns in each of those years, but the difference was not statistically significant.

Table 10b displays the results for the greater-than-10 percent allocation threshold. This threshold provided the most dramatic evidence of a return premium using just 2006 allocation targets. Pensions allocating at least 10 percent of their portfolio to alternative assets in 2001 and 2006 show significantly higher returns in 2005 and 2006, but significantly lower returns in 2003. When we increase the allocation threshold to 15 percent, as shown in table 10c, 2005 and 2006 still show significantly higher returns, but 2003 is no longer significantly lower.[20] Indeed, at the 15 percent allocation threshold, the lower returns in 2002 and 2003 decrease to just 10 and 25 basis points, respectively.

Together, the results in tables 10a through 10c suggest that pension plans that have had investments in alternative assets of 10 percent or 15 percent since at least 2001 had significantly higher returns in 2005 and 2006. These higher returns also helped increase the 3-year, 5-year, and 10-year average returns for these pension plans to significant or nearly significant differences. Thus, these results provide mixed evidence for the idea of performance rewards for pensions making sizeable long-term investments in alternative assets. For pensions with an older vintage to their alternative asset allocation, returns were higher from 2004 through 2006, but remained lower in 2002 and 2003.

When we look at our measures of risk and risk-adjusted returns for pensions that adopted an alternative asset allocation target as early as 2001, our results are again somewhat similar to our previous results. As table 11 shows, the standard deviations of

---

[20] We do not consider the 20 percent allocation level in these tests because only one pension plan had such an allocation level in 2001.

returns over our five-year period are higher for the pensions with the early commitment to alternative assets. However, the differences are only significantly higher at the 10 percent allocation threshold. Looking at the comparison of the Sharpe Ratios in table 12, we find an outcome very similar to our earlier results: no evidence of significant differences in risk-adjusted returns between the two pension groups.

As another check on the robustness of our results, we look at the early adoption of alternative asset allocations, but only for the subset of 22 pensions that had an allocation target of at least 10 percent in 2006. For more evidence of a benefit to a long term commitment to alternative assets, we would like to see pension plans with such a commitment outperform plans with similar alternative asset allocations but with a more recent adoption of this allocation, i.e., after 2001. Table 13 shows test results comparing pension plans with an alternative asset allocation target of at least 10 percent in both 2001 and 2006 with pension plans that had a target of at least 10 percent in 2006 but less than 10 percent in 2001. Of course, because they do eventually have similar allocation targets, we do not expect the two groups to differ significantly at the three short horizons we consider: 2005, 2006, and the three-year average. However, as table 13 shows, we do not find evidence of superior returns at any of our time horizons. As the results in table 13 make clear, the pension plans with the longer commitment to alternative assets do not have significantly higher returns than pension plans that dedicated assets to alternative investments more recently. The difference in the means even shows that the long-term alternative investment pension plans had lower average returns in 2002, 2003, and 2004, but these differences are not significant.

Together, the results from tables 10 through 13 provide little evidence of a benefit to a longer term allocation to alternative investments over our sample period. The results in table 13 in particular, suggest that most of the superior returns garnered by pension plans with relatively large portfolio allocations to alternative investments came from strong returns from alternative assets over the past three years. While these results suggest that the performance of alternative investments over the past three years has been impressive, a much stronger showing at the five-year and 10-year horizons would have done much to argue in favor of alternative assets as an essential permanent component of a pension portfolio.

Performance Comparison by 2006 Hedge Fund Allocation

Although only seven of our 39 pension plans reported hedge fund investments greater than zero, we are able to compare the mean investment returns of plans with and without these assets. Table 14a shows the results of our investment return comparisons between plans with hedge fund investments and those without hedge funds. Although the mean return of the group investing in hedge funds is higher for the period 2004 through 2006 and lower in 2002 and 2003, our p-values show that none of these differences are significant. Our equality of variance test suggests that there is no difference in the variances of the returns of the two groups after 2003. When we increase the hedge fund target threshold to at least 5 percent, only returns during the years 2002 and 2004 were significantly different. Of course, we don't know whether any pension plans were investing in hedge funds as early as 2002 because we only have hedge fund data for

2006. Returns at pensions with a hedge fund allocation in 2006 are higher from 2004 through 2006

Although our test results suggest that allocating at least 10 percent of your portfolio to alternative investments may have a significant effect on investments returns, those results do not suggest any significant effect from allocating a given amount to hedge funds specifically. Of course, hedge fund investments are fairly new to public pension plans, so it will be important to see whether these results change over time before we come to any definitive conclusion about the effect of hedge funds on public pension plan performance. At present, however, we find little evidence that hedge funds significantly benefit or harm public pension fund returns. We find that there is no significant difference in investment performance over any of the investment periods for the seven pension plans that had hedge fund investments greater than zero in 2006. Pension plans with at least 5 percent allocated to hedge funds had significantly higher returns only in 2004, a year that we cannot confirm that the pensions actually targeted hedge funds.

V. Conclusion

Overseers of a public pension plan establish the plan's investment policy and asset allocation targets. For many pension plans these allocations include targets of 10 percent or more for alternative assets, which we define to include real estate, private equity, hedge funds, and a few other investments. Because public pension plans hold assets for our teachers, police officers, fire fighters, and other state and local government workers, we understand why the riskiness of alternative assets might raise concerns regarding the appropriateness of these assets in public pension fund portfolios. Our

23

approach to addressing these concerns is to look at how investing in alternative assets has affected the performance of a sample of public pension plans.

Comparing investment returns of 39 public pension plans, we find that pension plans with alternative asset target allocations of at least 10 percent but less than 20 percent had significantly higher returns than other pension plans at most of the investment horizons we examine. These investment horizons are individual years from 2002 through 2006, and average returns for the three-year, five-year, and 10-year periods ending June 30, 2006. Not only were the returns higher but also the return variances were about the same as for the other pension plans. (Most variances did not differ significantly.)

However, when we look to another measure of risk, namely the standard deviations of returns at individual pension plans, we find that the standard deviations of returns were consistently and significantly higher at pensions investing at least 10 percent of their assets in alternative assets. From this perspective, those pension plans were consistently riskier. Combining the two to look at risk-adjusted returns via the Sharpe Ratio, we find no significant difference in risk-adjusted returns regardless of the alternative asset allocation target. Together, these results suggest that investments in alternative assets brought higher returns over the past few years, but at the cost of greater volatility. It is up to pension fund managers and plan fiduciaries to determine whether the lure of attractive returns outweighs the accompanying increase in return variance.

Although our results provide some evidence in favor of including alternative assets in an investment portfolio if one is seeking higher returns, this endorsement comes with several caveats. First, we need to see how our pension plans perform over the next

24

three to five years before being completely persuaded that alternative investments provide significantly higher long-term returns to pension portfolios. In addition to seeing how alternative investments perform through the market turmoil that began around June 2007, the additional data is also important in light of our tests showing that early and late adopters of alternative asset allocations did not show significantly different returns. These results suggest that most of the benefits of alternative investments came from their strong performance over just the past three years. Pension fund fiduciaries might like to see more evidence of a benefit to long-term investing in alternative assets before dedicating a larger percentage of their assets to these investments.

Another caveat is in order because of the additional risks associated with alternative investments. Because of possible liquidity and disclosure problems, it is absolutely crucial for a public pension plan to have a thorough due diligence effort in place to pick the right alternative investment and to consider the potential operational risks and hazards that these investments pose. Hedge funds, in particular, with their self-regulation, lockup periods, a lack of disclosure that seems to increase the opportunity for fraud, and other perils, provide a good example of why superior due diligence is a critical need for pension funds that elect to target alternative investments.

Another concern that may emerge over time is how to deal with performance-based compensation for public pension fund managers. This issue recently arose in Massachusetts when the director of the state pension fund asked for and received a performance-based bonus plan. Public plans with performance-based compensation features now include California, Maryland, Massachusetts, Texas and South Dakota.[21]

---

[21] See Frank Phillips, "Pension Director Looks for Bonuses," *The Boston Globe*, August 8, 2007 and Andrea Estes, "Bonus Plan Approved for Pension Fund Employees," *The Boston Globe*, October 3, 2007.

Our results show that large allocations for alternative assets may provide significantly higher returns in individual years (for instance, over 300 basis points in 2006). However, at investment horizons of five and ten years, the higher returns tend to be much less dramatic — for example, 102 basis points over five years and 76 basis points over 10 years for pension funds with at least a 10 percent target allocation for alternative assets in 2006 (see table 7b). What these results suggest is that public pension fund trustees should be aware that performance-based compensation packages may give fund directors an incentive to swing for the fences with larger allocations for alternative investments even though the pension fund's long-term benefits from such an investment strategy remains in doubt.

With these caveats in mind, our results do suggest that alternative assets are important investments for pension plans. In light of the turmoil in credit markets in 2007 and how often the business news mentions our alternative assets, namely real estate, private equity, and hedge funds, in connection with this market turmoil, it will be interesting to see how alternative investments and our results regarding them withstand the tests of time and market upheaval.

If maintained, our evidence of superior returns because of alternative assets suggests that a rather striking policy reassessment may be in order. If large allocations for alternative assets produce significantly higher returns over a longer time period, as our evidence suggests, then alternative assets may be an important component of any retirement fund portfolio. If this is true, then policy makers may want to consider ways to make alternative assets, including possibly even hedge funds, more easily available to defined contribution retirement plan participants. As defined contribution plans like

26

401(k) plans continue to replace defined benefit plans, fewer workers are covered by defined benefit plans like those in our study. While defined benefit plans can easily invest in alternative assets, defined contribution plans usually cannot. But if alternative assets are important components of diversified defined benefit portfolios, the same may be true for individual retirement accounts and defined contribution plan portfolios.[22]

---

[22] There is anecdotal evidence that some defined contribution plans are already moving into alternative investments; see Segal (2007).

References

Ackermann, Carl, Richard McEnally, and David Ravenscraft, 1999, "The Performance of Hedge Funds: Risk Return, and Incentives," *The Journal of Finance*, Vol. 54, No. 3 (June 1999), pp. 833-874.

Blake, David, Bruce N. Lehmann, and Allan Timmermann, 1999, "Asset Allocation Dynamics and Pension Fund Performance," *The Journal of Business*, Vol. 72, No. 4, October 1999, pp. 429-461.

Brinson, Gary P., L. Randolph Hood, and Gilbert L. Beebower, 1986, "Determinants of Portfolio Performance," *Financial Analysts Journal*, July-August 1986, pp. 39-44.

Brull, Steven, 2007, "Cap and Frown," *Institutional Investor*, September 2007, pp. 128-134.

Brull, Steven, 2008, "Raising the Stakes," *Institutional Investor*, February 2008, pp. 34-39.

Barber, Felix, and Michael Goold, 2007, "The Strategic Secret of Private Equity," *Harvard Business Review*, September 2007, pp. 53-61.

Berkowitz, Stephen A., Louis D. Finney and Dennis E. Logue, 1988, *The Investment Performance of Corporate Pension Plans*, New York: Quorum Books.

Brown, Stephen J., and William N. Goetzmann, 1995, "Performance Persistence," *The Journal of Finance*, Vol. 50, No. 2, June 1995, 679-698.

Coggin, T. Daniel, Frank J. Fabozzi and Shafiqur Rahman, 1993, "The Investment Performance of U.S. Equity Pension Fund Managers: An Empirical Investigation," *The Journal of Finance*, Vol. 48, No. 3, July 1993, pp. 1039-1055.

Craft, Timothy M., 2001, "The Role of Private and Public Real Estate in Pension Plan Portfolio Allocation Choices," *Journal of Real Estate Portfolio Management*, Vol. 7, No. 1, pp. 17-23.

Denmark, Frances, 2007, "Making the Grade," *Institutional Investor*, August 2007, pp. 53-58.

Elton, Edwin J., and Martin J. Gruber, 2000, "The Rationality of Asset Allocation Recommendations," *The Journal of Financial and Quantitative Analysis*, Vo. 35, No. 1, March 2000, pp. 27-41.

Fama, Eugene F., 1972, "Components of Investment Performance," *The Journal of Finance*, Vol. 27, No. 3, June 1972, pp. 551-567.

Gregorious, Greg N., and Fabrice Rouah, 2002, "The Role of Hedge Funds in Pension Fund Portfolios: Buying Protection in Bear Markets," *Journal of Pensions Management*, Vol. 7, No. 3 (April 2002), pp. 237-245.

Ippolito, R. A., and J. A. Turner, 1987, "Turnover Fees and Pension Plan Performance," *Financial Analysts Journal*, Vol. 43, No. 6, pp. 16-26.

Kambhu, John, Til Schuermann, and Kevin J. Stiroh, 2007, "Hedge Funds, Financial Intermediation, and Systemic Risk," Federal Reserve Bank of New York Staff Reports, No. 291, July 2007.

Klunk, William, 2007, "Pension Funds Investing in Hedge Funds," Congressional Research Service, June 15, 2007.

Maggs, Amy J., 2006, "State Pension Funds Are Hedging Their Bets," *Benefits Law Journal*, Vol. 19, No. 3 (Autumn 2006), pp. 70-79.

Pozen, Robert C., 2007, "If Private Equity Sized Up Your Business," *Harvard Business Review*, November 2007, pp. 78-87.

Segal, Julie, 2007, "Alternative Retirement Plans," *Institutional Investor*, September 2007, p. 213.

Sharpe, William F., 1994, "The Sharpe Ratio," *The Journal of Portfolio Management*, Fall 1994.

Steenburg, Thomas N. and Amy J. Maggs, 2007, "Monitoring Hedge Fund Investments: What's a Good Fiduciary to Do?" *Benefits Law Journal*, Vol. 20, No. 2 (Summer 2007), pp. 65-80.

Tokat, Yesim, Nelson Wicas, and Francis M. Kinniry, 2006, "The Asset Allocation Debate: A Review and Reconciliation," *Journal of Financial Planning*, October 2006.

Walsh, Mary Williams and Riva D. Atlas, "Pension, Hedge-Fund Ties a Concern," *The Seattle Times*, November 27, 2005.

Table 1. Pension Fund Asset Allocation Targets, Selected States, June 30, 2006.

Asset Class	California Public Employees' Retirement System	State Employees' Retirement System of Illinois[23]	State Retirement and Pension System of Maryland[24]
Domestic Equity	40%	45%	40%
International Equity	20%	10%	13%
Global Equity[25]			10%
Global Debt Securities	26%	25%	30%
Alternative Investments	6%	10%	2%
Real Estate	8%	10%	5%
Total	100%	100%	100%

Table 2. Summary Statistics of Public Pension Plan Sample, 2006

Variable	N	Total	Mean	Median
Membership	51	13,379,424	262,342	162,352
Investment Values				
Total Assets	51	$1,684.4 bil.	$33.0 bil.	$16.0 bil.
Equity	50	$876.9 bil.	$17.5 bil.	$9.0 bil.
Fixed Income	50	$405.5 bil.	$8.1 bil.	$4.1 bil.
Real Estate	39	$67.4 bil.	$1.7 bil.	$0.8 bil.
Alternatives	36	$74.4 bil.	$2.1 bil.	$0.8 bil.
Hedge Funds	9	$6.1 bil.	$0.7 bil.	$0.4 bil.

[23] The policy target for the State Employees' Retirement System of Illinois allocates 5 percent to U.S. equity hedge funds and 5 percent to private equity. We combine these two allocations into the Alternative Asset category.

[24] The policy target for the State Retirement and Pension System of Maryland allocates 28 percent to fixed income and 2 percent to a real return asset class that generally invests in inflation protection securities. We combine these two allocations into the global debt securities category.

[25] Global investments include U.S. and non-U.S. investments, whereas international investments include just non-U.S. investments.

Table 3. Mean Asset Allocation Targets in 2001 and 2006

Investment	N		2001 Target		2006 Target	
	2001	2006	Mean	Std. Dev.	Mean	Std. Dev.
Equity	51	51	57.2	9.0	58.6	6.6
Fixed Income	51	51	34.9	11.7	29.5	7.0
Real Estate	31	36	5.7	3.0	6.3	2.5
Alternatives	32	36	7.0	4.4	7.9	4.4
Real Estate and Alternatives Combined	37	45	10.8	6.0	12.3	6.4
Hedge Funds	0	7	NA	NA	3.5	2.0

Table 4. Net Investment Returns, Plans Reporting as of June 30, 2006

Period	N	Mean	Std. Dev.	Min.	Max.
2002	39	-5.72%	1.99%	-9.00%	0.93%
2003	39	4.23%	1.60%	0.30%	8.88%
2004	39	15.37%	2.48%	8.76%	19.50%
2005	39	10.56%	1.76%	7.02%	14.07%
2006	39	10.84%	2.36%	5.13%	16.70%
3-year Average	39	12.23%	2.00%	6.96%	16.07%
5-year Average	39	6.81%	0.99%	4.70%	8.75%
10-year Average	26	8.67%	0.87%	6.86%	10.29%

31

Table 5. Common Benchmark Investment Results, Years Ending June 30
(Source: North Dakota Public Employees Retirement System 2006 Annual Report)

Asset	Year				
	2002	2003	2004	2005	2006
Domestic Large Cap: S&P 500	-17.99%	0.25%	19.11%	6.32%	8.63%
Domestic Small Cap: Russell 2000	-8.60%	-1.64%	33.37%	9.45%	14.58%
International Equities: MSCI 50% Hedged EAFE Index	-14.62%	-11.24%	25.74%	17.60%	26.72%
Emerging Markets Equities: MSCI Emerging Markets	1.31%	6.96%	33.51%	34.89%	35.91%
Domestic Fixed Income: Lehmann Brothers Aggregate	8.63%	10.40%	0.32%	6.80%	-0.81%
High Yield Bonds: Lehmann Brothers High Yield Bonds	-3.60%	22.76%	10.32%	10.86%	4.37%
International Fixed Income: %Citi World Government Non-US	15.73%	17.90%	7.60%	7.75%	-0.01%
Real Estate: NCREIF Index	5.52%	7.64%	10.82%	18.02%	18.67%
Private Equity[26]	-29.02%	-9.65%	3.23%	17.24%	11.08%
90 Day T-bills	2.63%	1.53%	0.98%	2.15%	3.98%

---

[26] Private equity does not have a common benchmark. These figures reflect the private equity investment results of the North Dakota Public Employees Retirement System

Table 6. Return Differences by 2006 Median Target Asset Allocations,
Years Ending June 30, Averages through June 30, 2006

2006 Allocation Threshold		Return Period							
		2002	2003	2004	2005	2006	3-year	5-year	10-year
Dom. Equity ≥ 42%	Mean Diff.	-1.2%	-0.4%	0.4%	-1.1%	-1.3%	-0.8%	**-0.8%**	-0.6%
	p-value	.0524	.3400	.6063	.0622	.0538	.1945	**.0085***	.0579
Int. Equity ≥ 18%	Mean Diff.	0.2%	0.1%	**1.4%**	**1.3%**	1.1%	**1.3%**	**0.8%**	0.3%
	p-value	.7607	.8422	**.0363***	**.0203***	.1011	**.0187***	**.0096***	.2911
Fixed Income ≥ 30%	Mean Diff.	**1.7%**	**1.6%**	**-2.3%**	**-1.1%**	**-2.7%**	**-2.1%**	-0.5%	-0.6%
	p-value	**.0056***	**.0016***	**.0017***	**.0497***	**.0001***	**.0006***	.1421	.1110
Alternatives ≥ 10%	Mean Diff.	-0.7%	-0.8%	**2.0%**	**2.1%**	**3.0%**	**2.4%**	**1.0%**	**0.8%**
	p-value	.3384	.1043	**.0154***	**<.0001***	**<.0001***	**<.0001***	**.0007***	**.0235***

33

Table 7a. Mean Investment Return Comparison: 2006 Alternative Target > 0 %

Return Period	2006 Alt. Target Allocation > 0 %			2006 Alt. Target Allocation = 0 %			Mean Diff.	p-value Mean Diff.	Var. Diff. Pr > F
	N	Mean	SD	N	Mean	SD			
2002	34	-6.15	1.53	5	-2.79	2.44	-3.36	.0001*	.1156
2003	34	4.03	1.48	5	5.54	2.00	-1.50	.0489*	.2909
2004	34	15.76	2.14	5	12.66	3.16	3.10	.0072*	.1863
2005	34	10.76	1.70	5	9.17	1.66	1.59	.0585	1.000
2006	34	11.24	2.07	5	8.11	2.63	3.13	.0042*	.3911
3 Yrs	34	12.56	1.74	5	9.97	2.39	2.60	.0052*	.2705
5 Yrs	34	6.87	0.97	5	6.42	1.14	0.45	.3487	.5257
10 Yrs	24	8.69	0.79	2	8.38	2.15	0.31	.8712	.0240[27]

Table 7b. Mean Investment Return Comparison: 2006 Alternative Target ≥ 10%

Return Period	2006 Alt. Target Allocation ≥ 10%			2006 Alt. Target Allocation < 10%			Mean Diff.	p-value Mean Diff.	Var. Diff. Pr > F
	N	Mean	SD	N	Mean	SD			
2002	22	-6.02	1.16	17	-5.33	2.71	-0.69	.3384	.0004
2003	22	3.86	1.44	17	4.70	1.72	-0.84	.1043	.4367
2004	22	16.25	1.77	17	14.22	2.83	2.03	.0154*	.0463
2005	22	11.46	1.53	17	9.39	1.32	2.07	<.0001*	.5578
2006	22	12.16	1.69	17	9.13	2.00	3.03	<.0001*	.4739
3 Yrs	22	13.27	1.44	17	10.89	1.84	2.39	<.0001*	.2900
5 Yrs	22	7.26	0.89	17	6.24	0.80	1.02	.0007*	.6567
10 Yrs	14	9.02	0.73	12	8.26	0.87	0.76	.0235*	.5538

Table 7c. Mean Investment Return Comparison: 2006 Alternative Target ≥ 20%

Return Period	2006 Alt. Target Allocation ≥ 20%			2006 Alt. Target Allocation < 20%			Mean Diff.	p-value Mean Diff.	Var. Diff. Pr > F
	N	Mean	SD	N	Mean	SD			
2002	6	-6.31	0.47	33	-5.61	2.14	-0.70	.1019	.0031
2003	6	3.66	2.17	33	4.33	1.50	-0.67	.3528	.1840
2004	6	17.01	1.54	33	15.07	2.51	1.95	.0766	.2755
2005	6	12.01	1.99	33	10.30	1.61	1.72	.0261*	.4190
2006	6	13.45	2.37	33	10.37	2.06	3.09	.0021*	.5574
3 Yrs	6	14.15	1.74	33	11.88	1.86	2.26	.0090*	.9806
5 Yrs	6	7.63	1.18	33	6.66	0.89	0.97	.0250*	.2929
10 Yrs	4	9.36	0.81	22	8.54	0.84	0.82	.0850	1.000

[27] When our F-test rejects the hypothesis of equal variance, we use the Satterthwaite method t-test as opposed to the usual pooled method.

34

Table 8. Comparison of Standard Deviations of 2002-2006 Returns by 2006 Alternative Investment Targets

2006 Alternative Assets Threshold	2006 Alternative Investment Target At Threshold			2006 Alternative Investment Target Below Threshold			Mean Diff.	p-value for Mean Diff.	Var. Diff. Pr > F
	N	Mean STD	SD	N	Mean STD	SD			
> 0%	34	8.59	1.30	5	6.00	1.63	2.59	.0003*	.4075
≥ 5 %	30	8.67	1.11	9	6.89	2.17	1.78	.0408*	.0076
≥ 10 %	22	8.85	1.07	17	7.49	1.84	1.36	.0122*	.0225
≥ 15 %	10	9.11	0.95	29	7.96	1.67	1.15	.0466*	.0783
≥ 20 %	6	9.44	0.87	33	8.04	1.60	1.40	.0460*	.1766

Table 9. 2002-2006 Sharpe Ratio Comparison, by 2006 Alternative Investment Targets

2006 Alternative Assets Threshold	2006 Alternative Investment Target At Threshold			2006 Alternative Investment Target Below Threshold			Mean Diff.	p-value for Mean Diff.	Var. Diff. Pr > F
	N	Mean Sharpe	SD	N	Mean Sharpe	SD			
> 0 %	34	.556	.097	5	.683	.208	-.127	.2455	.0089
≥ 5 %	30	.563	.092	9	.601	.193	-.038	.5820	.0030
≥ 10 %	22	.586	.083	17	.554	.158	.032	.4625	.0064
≥ 15 %	10	.586	.105	29	.567	.127	.019	.6815	.5688
≥ 20 %	6	.592	.098	33	.568	.126	.024	.6668	.6092

Table 10a. Mean Investment Return Comparison:
2001 & 2006 Alternative Investment Targets > 0%

Return Period	Alt. Target Allocation > 0 %			Alt. Target Allocation = 0 %			Mean Diff.	p-value Mean Diff.	Var. Diff. Pr > F
	N	Mean	SD	N	Mean	SD			
2002	28	-5.97	1.48	11	-5.09	2.91	-0.88	.3575	.0047
2003	28	3.96	1.46	11	4.90	1.83	-0.94	.1015	.3390
2004	28	15.71	2.29	11	14.50	2.84	1.20	.1752	.3615
2005	28	10.88	1.72	11	9.74	1.67	1.15	.0665	.9817
2006	28	11.51	2.12	11	9.14	2.17	2.37	.0035*	.8683
3 Yrs	28	12.68	1.86	11	11.10	1.97	1.58	.0242*	.7679
5 Yrs	28	6.96	0.94	11	6.45	1.05	0.51	.1475	.6188
10 Yrs	18	8.81	0.81	8	8.35	0.98	0.45	.2302	.4980

Table 10b. Mean Investment Return Comparison:
2001 & 2006 Alternative Investment Targets ≥ 10%

Return Period	Alt. Target Allocation ≥ 10 %			Alt. Target Allocation < 10 %			Mean Diff.	p-value Mean Diff.	Var. Diff. Pr > F
	N	Mean	SD	N	Mean	SD			
2002	16	-6.72	1.17	23	-5.46	2.39	-0.64	.2766	.0062
2003	16	3.60	1.46	23	4.67	1.58	-1.07	.0387*	.7533
2004	16	15.99	1.79	23	14.93	2.82	1.06	.1918	.0764
2005	16	11.56	1.60	23	9.86	1.54	1.70	.0019*	.8538
2006	16	12.21	1.99	23	9.89	2.16	2.32	.0016*	.7639
3 Yrs	16	13.24	1.63	23	11.53	1.96	1.72	.0067*	.4554
5 Yrs	16	7.16	0.99	23	6.57	0.93	0.59	.0637	.7610
10 Yrs	10	9.12	0.78	16	8.39	0.83	0.73	.0358*	.8661

Table 10c. Mean Investment Return Comparison:
2001 & 2006 Alternative Investment Targets ≥ 15%

Return Period	Alt. Target Allocation ≥ 15 %			Alt. Target Allocation < 15 %			Mean Diff.	p-value Mean Diff.	Var. Diff. Pr > F
	N	Mean	SD	N	Mean	SD			
2002	5	-5.81	0.81	34	-5.71	2.11	-0.10	.9176	.0736
2003	5	4.01	1.35	34	4.26	1.65	-0.25	.7470	.7570
2004	5	15.93	1.57	34	15.28	2.59	0.65	.5896	.3394
2005	5	12.40	1.45	34	10.29	1.65	2.11	.0103*	.8942
2006	5	13.15	2.49	34	10.50	2.18	2.65	.0169*	.5740
3 Yrs	5	13.85	1.70	34	11.99	1.95	1.85	.0518	.8796
5 Yrs	5	7.71	1.03	34	6.68	0.92	1.03	.0273*	.6216
10 Yrs	4	9.46	0.71	22	8.52	0.83	0.93	.0479*	.9088

Table 11. Comparison of Standard Deviation of 2002-2006 Returns by 2001 and 2006 Alternative Investment Targets

2001 & 2006 Alternative Assets Threshold	Alternative Investment Targets At Threshold			Alternative Investment Targets Below Threshold			Mean Diff.	p-value for Mean Diff.	Var. Diff. Pr > F
	N	Mean STD	SD	N	Mean STD	SD			
> 0 %	28	8.55	1.41	11	7.51	1.83	1.04	.0637	.2753
≥ 5 %	24	8.69	1.06	15	7.57	2.04	1.11	.0661	.0056
≥ 10 %	16	8.86	1.15	23	7.84	1.73	1.02	.0471*	.1075
≥ 15 %	5	8.92	1.05	34	8.16	1.64	0.76	.3215	.4011

Table 12. 2002-2006 Sharpe Ratio Comparison, by 2001 and 2006 Alternative Investment Targets

2001 & 2006 Alternative Assets Threshold	Alternative Investment Targets At Threshold			Alternative Investment Targets Below Threshold			Mean Diff.	p-value for Mean Diff.	Var. Diff. Pr > F
	N	Mean Sharpe	SD	N	Mean Sharpe	SD			
> 0 %	28	.569	.086	11	.581	.188	-.012	.8373	.0011
≥ 5 %	24	.567	.091	15	.580	.161	-.013	.7764	.0147
≥ 10 %	16	.576	.090	23	.569	.140	.007	.8684	.0777
≥ 15 %	5	.625	.089	34	.564	.124	.061	.2968	.5475

Table 13. Mean Investment Return Comparison: Early Alternative Asset Adopters (2001 & 2006 Alt. Target ≥ 10%) versus Later Adopters (Only 2006 Alt. Target ≥ 10%)

Return Period	2001& 2006 Alt. Target Allocation ≥ 10%			Only 2006 Alt. Target Allocation ≥ 10%			Mean Diff.	p-value Mean Diff.	Var. Diff. Pr > F
	N	Mean	SD	N	Mean	SD			
2002	16	-6.10	1.17	6	-5.81	1.21	-0.28	.6227	.8244
2003	16	3.60	1.46	6	4.56	1.24	-0.97	.1662	.7601
2004	16	15.99	1.79	6	16.95	1.65	-0.95	.2703	.9268
2005	16	11.56	1.60	6	11.20	1.41	0.37	.6269	.8374
2006	16	12.21	1.99	6	12.04	0.40	0.17	.7546	.0023
3 Yrs	16	13.24	1.63	6	13.35	0.87	-0.11	.8802	.1746
5 Yrs	16	7.16	0.99	6	7.51	0.55	-0.35	.4261	.1951
10 Yrs	10	9.12	0.78	4	8.78	0.64	0.34	.4582	.8298

Table 14a. Mean Investment Return Comparison: 2006 Hedge Fund Investments > 0%

Return Period	2006 Hedge Fund Asset Share > 0%			2006 Hedge Fund Asset Share = 0%			Mean Diff.	p-value Mean Diff.	Var. Diff. Pr > F
	N	Mean	SD	N	Mean	SD			
2002	7	-6.11	0.90	32	-5.63	2.15	-0.48	.3602	.0356
2003	7	4.18	2.50	32	4.24	1.40	-0.06	.9555	.0285
2004	7	16.56	2.43	32	15.10	2.45	1.46	.1620	1.000
2005	7	11.02	1.65	32	10.46	1.79	0.56	.4555	.9114
2006	7	11.60	2.43	32	10.67	2.35	0.93	.3538	.8068
3 Yrs	7	13.01	1.98	32	12.06	2.00	0.95	.2611	1.000
5 Yrs	7	7.14	1.04	32	6.74	0.98	0.40	.3379	.7417
10 Yrs	4	8.96	1.02	22	8.61	0.86	0.35	.4788	.5423

Table 14b. Mean Investment Return Comparison: 2006 Hedge Fund Target ≥ 5%

Return Period	2006 Hedge Fund Target ≥ 5%			2006 Hedge Fund Target < 5%			Mean Diff.	p-value Mean Diff.	Var. Diff. Pr > F
	N	Mean	SD	N	Mean	SD			
2002	4	-6.73	0.48	35	-5.60	2.06	-1.12	.0150*	.0335
2003	4	3.46	2.81	35	4.31	1.45	-0.86	.5886	.0389
2004	4	17.71	1.30	35	15.10	2.45	2.61	.0445*	.3248
2005	4	12.03	1.41	35	10.39	1.73	1.64	.0777	.8322
2006	4	12.59	2.00	35	10.64	2.34	1.95	.1188	.9201
3 Yrs	4	14.04	1.52	35	12.02	1.96	2.02	.0548	.7624
5 Yrs	4	7.44	1.29	35	6.74	0.94	0.70	.1850	.3112
10 Yrs	3	9.28	0.97	23	8.59	0.85	0.69	.2033	.5858

Table 15a. Mean Investment Return Comparison: 2006 Alternative Actual > 0 %

Return Period	2006 Alt. Actual Allocation > 0 %			2006 Alt. Actual Allocation = 0 %			Mean Diff.	p-value Mean Diff.	Var. Diff. Pr > F
	N	Mean	SD	N	Mean	SD			
2002	34	-6.15	1.53	5	-2.79	2.44	-3.36	.0001*	.1156
2003	34	4.03	1.48	5	5.54	2.00	-1.50	.0489*	.2909
2004	34	15.76	2.14	5	12.66	3.16	3.10	.0072*	.1863
2005	34	10.76	1.70	5	9.17	1.66	1.59	.0585	1.000
2006	34	11.24	2.07	5	8.11	2.63	3.13	.0042*	.3911
3 Yrs	34	12.56	1.74	5	9.97	2.39	2.60	.0052*	.2705
5 Yrs	34	6.87	0.97	5	6.42	1.14	0.45	.3487	.5257
10 Yrs	24	8.69	0.79	2	8.38	2.15	0.31	.8712	.0240

Table 15b. Mean Investment Return Comparison: 2006 Alternative Actual ≥ 10%

Return Period	2006 Alt. Actual Allocation ≥ 10%			2006 Alt. Actual Allocation < 10%			Mean Diff.	p-value Mean Diff.	Var. Diff. Pr > F
	N	Mean	SD	N	Mean	SD			
2002	12	-5.98	0.63	27	-5.60	2.36	-0.38	.4481	<.0001
2003	12	3.76	1.67	27	4.43	1.56	-0.67	.2303	.7280
2004	12	16.33	1.46	27	14.93	2.72	1.41	.0444*	.0348
2005	12	11.69	1.63	27	10.06	1.60	1.64	.0057*	.8904
2006	12	12.52	2.01	27	10.09	2.14	2.43	.0020*	.8694
3 Yrs	12	13.51	1.54	27	11.67	1.94	1.84	.0063*	.4185
5 Yrs	12	7.37	1.07	27	6.57	0.85	0.80	.0171*	.3297
10 Yrs	8	9.41	0.65	18	8.34	0.76	1.08	.0019*	.7130

Table 15c. Mean Investment Return Comparison: 2006 Alternative Actual ≥ 15%

Return Period	2006 Alt. Actual Allocation ≥ 15%			2006 Alt. Actual Allocation < 15%			Mean Diff.	p-value Mean Diff.	Var. Diff. Pr > F
	N	Mean	SD	N	Mean	SD			
2002	5	-6.30	0.52	34	-5.63	2.11	-0.66	.1356	.0146
2003	5	3.83	2.38	34	4.28	1.50	-0.45	.5612	.1199
2004	5	16.81	1.63	34	15.15	2.53	1.66	.1645	.4110
2005	5	11.67	2.02	34	10.40	1.69	1.28	.1315	.4895
2006	5	13.28	2.61	34	10.48	2.14	2.80	.0113*	.4552
3 Yrs	5	13.91	1.84	34	11.98	1.93	1.93	.0424*	1.000
5 Yrs	5	7.54	1.30	34	6.71	0.91	0.83	.0781	.2232
10 Yrs	4	9.36	0.81	22	8.54	0.84	0.82	.0850	1.000

www.ingramcontent.com/pod-product-compliance
Lightning Source LLC
Chambersburg PA
CBHW060442290526
45793CB00002B/542